*Merry Christmas Anne*
*from Betty*
*Dec. 2009*

# Tales From the Teapot
### Hidden Treasures found in the History of Tea

## Dolly Yates

*Sincerely,*
*Dolly Yates.*

# Acknowledgements

My very grateful thanks to my niece Pauline who painstakingly proofread my manuscript and enters it into Microsoft format.

My grateful thanks to Anthea M. Davies for all her helpful suggestions as she willingly reviewed my work.

I gave Cliff Baxendale a word picture of my story of the miner and he very graciously portrayed a perfect image in black and white of every detail described to him. I do thank him so very much for this splendid piece of artwork.

Many friends and family have been very encouraging and supportive, that has meant a lot to me and I do thank each one of you so much.

My last acknowledgment is for my granddaughter Miriam, who I can only describe as my right arm throughout the whole procedure of getting this book together. There was so much that I would not have been able to handle myself in these days of high technology. Miriam gave her time unstintingly to me at all times. Thank you so very much sweet Miriam, you are a treasure.


Dolly Yates

## Dedication

I dedicate this book to my daughter in law Lesley
who drinks more cups of tea in one day
than anyone I know.

Dear reader,

I sit and ponder just what is it that compels me, at my great age of 88, to attempt to write a narrative on such a commonplace thing as tea.

Looking back, it all began a few years earlier when I was invited to give a talk about tea at a Ladies' Afternoon Tea. At first I was quite taken aback at the thought. Here I was, English born and bred, drinking tea all my life without ever giving the subject a single thought. To me it was just like breathing, you just do it, nothing to it. Then my mind began to tick over and the more I thought about it, the more I realized there was a great deal to say about tea. So I accepted the invitation to give the "Tea Talk" and since then I have been able to repeat this on numerous occasions. The last one I gave was in my 88th year and it was at this time I began to have insights into the many spiritual truths linked to the story of tea.

I felt in my heart a great compulsion to share these thoughts as I spoke at my last "Tea Talk". As anyone can tell you, who has done any public speaking, it can be physically draining and so I felt that at my age it could be my very last "Tea Talk".

I decided to ask the president of the ladies if it would be in order for me to include my spiritual insights in my talk. Her answer was, "By all means." It certainly was a fulfilling experience and I'm glad I listened to my heart.

It is with the very same compulsion that I have attempted to put this narrative together so that you, dear reader, may receive some eternal truth from the lowly and simple "cup o' tea".

Dolly Yates May 17, 2008

# Table of Contents

# Chapter 1

## Messed up tea leaves

It never comes as a surprise, the incredible antics of a two year old. This is just the place to tell you of one of those antics of my two year old son. Whatever it was that we were busy doing, sure enough, baby Paul was always right there lending a hand. Sometimes this could be a little discomforting as I will relate.

My husband was busy mixing royal icing to ice a wedding cake. As usual, toddler Paul had taken up his position on a chair as close to operations as possible. It so happened I had just deposited the contents of a packet of tea into the tea caddy, leaving the empty packet on the table whilst replacing the tea caddy lid. Almost before you could blink an eye, young Paul quickly picked up the empty packet and shook it vigorously over the bowl of icing mixture. Obviously he had been observing how his dad shook portions of confectioner's sugar into the mixture.

We were a little dismayed when we viewed the several specks of tea leaves scattered over the icing and already it was showing tinges of pale brown as the moisture drew out the color from the leaves. In ordinary circumstances this would not have been a problem; we could have thrown the whole thing out and started again. Unfortunately this was wartime 1943 and sugar was severely rationed. The confectioner's sugar for the cake had been donated sacrificially by the family of the bride and groom. There was simply no way more sugar could be acquired in time.

Our little son had a very good motive for pitching in the remnants of the tea packet; he innocently thought it was sugar. Clearly, tea was never intended to be used that way.

Who among us, at different times in our lives, has messed up in some way or other? At such times we need to remember we have a loving Heavenly Father who sees and understands as no one else ever can. Of course, my son Paul can now make a perfect cup of tea. So may we, as we mature, learn from our past mistakes and go on to greater maturity.

# Chapter 2

## Camellia Sinensis

Try repeating Camellia Sinensis several times and it quickly becomes a tongue twister. I find it much easier to say a cup of tea than a cup of Camellia Sinensis. Now I am ready to reveal just what is Camellia Sinensis. It is a plant that thrives in South East Asia, the mountainous regions of Kenya, Sri Lanka and India and can grow to a height of 30 feet. The leaves grow all year round. It is related to the camellia plant and possesses flowers of outstanding beauty and perfume.

It is a well known fact that tea was drunk in China many centuries before it came to the notice of the rest of the world. Tea, like so many discoveries, happened by accident. The story goes that in the days of early Chinese civilization an emperor went on a journey. This emperor was ahead of his time so much so that he insisted his drinking water should always be boiled. While he was waiting a leaf from the tree Camellia Sinensis floated down and settled in the water. He decided to taste it, lo and behold we have the very first cup of tea!

For whatever reason, best known to them, the Chinese called the newly discovered beverage "chia" or in English, tea. Tea has always been tea; it is still tea today and will be tea tomorrow.

There are many beverages on the market today labeled as herbal teas, spicy teas etc, but these have no link what-soever to tea as it was, now is and always will be. All of these drinks are very pleasant to drink but do not possess any known physical benefits other than being caffeine free, whereas tea has been scientifically proven to have health benefits, namely it lowers the risks of a heart attack by 40%. It also contains a powerful antioxidant which helps reduce the risk of cancer.

Tea is made only from the leaves of the Camellia Sinensis plant; the tip and top few leaves are harvested every day to make the best tea. Originally tea was drunk green and this is the purest form. It was prepared by first drying out the leaves then crushing them slightly. It was the Europeans who processed black tea. This was done by partially drying and partially fermenting the leaves.

Sometimes I ponder what it would be like to sit under the shade of the Camellia Sinensis tree and drink tea freshly brewed from freshly picked tea tips. To sit there enjoying the fragrance from the flowers and admire their beauty whilst sipping fresh tea is a very remote possibility, but I am deeply grateful that at least it is possible to have tea in its present form.

This all makes me think of our great creator, Almighty God, who has always been who always is and always will be. He is the only authentic God, there is no other or ever can be. There have been many so-called gods in the past and there are still many today. These may be able to give a feeling of wellbeing but can impart no real benefit to life. In the same way we are able to enjoy tea today through the drying process; it brings to my mind a very clear picture of what God our Eternal Father did by sending His own dear Son to earth. As the tea has to go through the process of being dried and torn, in like manner, Jesus Christ lived a blameless life and went to the cross allowing His body to be bruised and torn. God allowed this to happen so the world may receive healing from the curse of sin with cleansing for the heart. This is truly amazing love that God our Creator became our Savior, presenting Himself in such a way that all may come and have eternal life.

In the Gospel of John chapter 1 and verses 1& 2 we read these words: "In the beginning was the Word, and the Word was with God, and the Word was God. He was with God from the beginning". This establishes the authenticity of who God is. Further in John 1 verse 14 we read, "The Word became flesh and made His dwelling among us. We have seen His glory, the glory of the One and only, who came from the Father, full of grace and truth." I have been a tea drinker as far back as I can remember, but of one thing I am certain, I do remember well the very first day I was introduced to the Lord Jesus Christ. The date was September 3rd 1933; that is a long time ago. When I came to Him He entered my whole heart and life and I know the quality of my life is enriched because of all the life-giving benefits from daily trusting in Him.

# Chapter 3

## Tea introduced to the world

Centuries had passed before the outside world became aware of the existence of tea. This came about through some Japanese Buddhists who took some seeds of the Camellia Sinensis tree back to Japan. It was not too long before they were drinking green tea. Its popularity quickly spread throughout the land. Their tea drinking became a very leisurely, long drawn out ritual; in fact, it can only be described as an important ceremony with many regulations. Much later the ceremony developed into something more than first intended and this brought sorrow to the Buddhist priests. After a while they persisted in restoring it to its original observance.

In like manner, over the centuries, there have been times in Church history when error has crept in and the original truth of God's Word has been lost. But God has raised up those who have restored the truth to the Church. We need to hold fast to the Word of God, which was once delivered to us.

I know the tea ceremony is still a significant part of Chinese and Japanese culture. They still drink green tea and this is served in tiny porcelain cups which are without handles. I do not know if black tea is ever taken in these two countries.

During the 17th century the Portuguese had established a trading station at Macao where they were able to send home a few pounds of tea now and then. This was most acceptable to the few people who could afford to buy it.

Very small quantities began to arrive in England during the years of Oliver Cromwell's Protectorate. The Puritans did not approve of this delightful beverage in the same way they objected to anything that brought pleasure, believing it to be sinful. The importers stressed tea's medicinal benefits hoping this would allow tea to be brought into the country. However, this argument failed to change the opinion of the Cromwellian purists. It needed the restoration of the monarchy, namely the Merry Monarch, King Charles II, to make way for the flow of tea to England. His bride to be, the Portuguese Princess Catherine brought a large chest of tea as her dowry. You may be forgiven for thinking this was a lowly gift from someone of such high rank, but when I tell you that in those days tea was sold for the princely sum of £100 per pound you will see it was no mean gift.

It was only royalty and the highest aristocracy who could afford such luxury. We have come so far in this day of modern technology that it is hard to imagine the real cost involved in transporting anything from one part of the world to another in the 17th century. Travel by sea was by sailing ship with huge crews pulling on oars. Bearing in mind that vast oceans separated China from Europe, it would take many months for a return journey. Numerous sailing vessels never returned but succumbed to the ravages of unpredictable mighty oceans. Those who manned these ships were always at risk of losing their lives or being attacked by pirates wishing to plunder a returning ship laden with precious cargo.

# Chapter 4

## Tea Chests and Tea Caddies

The Tea Chest was the container in which tea was transported to the country of its destination. It was a wooden box about 30 inches square and would be lined with silver paper; today it is lined with silver foil. When full of tea it would be fastened down tightly with a wooden lid. This way the tea would be perfectly airtight, serving two purposes: preserving the full flavor of the tea and preventing it from absorbing any other flavors. Being well sealed kept it free from dampness from the sea's atmosphere.

Tea still comes in tea chests today and is usually transported straight to the tea merchants. Years ago I remember seeing chests of tea in the grocery stores. The smell was unforgettable. The grocer would package the tea on his premises and the empty tea chests were sold for 6 pennies. They were quickly snapped up because they could be very useful. Some people used them to make dog kennels.

When I was engaged to be married, my mother bought me a tea chest to use as a "bottom drawer". It was the custom in those days to start collecting things for your home and these were stored in your "bottom drawer". We bought some pretty chintz to cover it, so it looked quite attractive in my bedroom. I hardly think anyone makes use of an empty tea chest nowadays; I dare say many people have not even seen one. It does seem a pity that in general, people have lost the art of utilizing such items as it is an opportunity for expressing creativity with very little expenditure.

Now I shall move on to the subject of the tea caddy. I found one version of the word "caddy" very interesting. Mary, Queen of Scots enjoyed playing golf whilst living in

France. Naturally, the Queen would not be expected to carry around her own golf clubs so she enlisted an army cadet to do this task. In time the cadet became known as the queen's caddy. Sounds very plausible!

Another explanation is that the word "caddy" evolved from the Malaysian word "kadi", which means a carrying case. A popular remark when leaving a friend would be, "Well, I'll pick up my kadi and vanish". As a child, this saying always left me feeling puzzled, whatever could that mean? Now that I am so well advanced in years and having just discovered what "kadi" means, it all makes perfect sense.

In our modern day and age the word caddy has a very definite meaning. A caddy is a container which is designed to hold a specific article. This means, for example, a golf caddy is meant to carry golf clubs, a jewelry caddy is to carry jewelry, a tennis caddy is to carry a tennis racket, and so we could go on. The caddy we will focus on is the tea caddy. The most distinctive feature about every tea caddy is that it must be completely airtight. This has three purposes: to preserve the flavor, to prevent outside odors affecting the tea and to prevent the tea from becoming stale.

The best tea caddies were made out of rosewood, mahogany and maple and were not large because tea was bought in small quantities. Tea caddies were not just containers for tea but came in many and varied artistic designs. Some would have mother of pearl incorporated into their designs, others would have carvings embossed on them. Some would be square, rectangular or oval and some even had carved feet. Most tea caddies used to be locked and the key would be kept by the lady of the house to prevent any pilfering of the precious commodity. Some tea caddies had two or three lids. After removing the top lid there could be a dividing lid which would cover two different sections each housing their own brand of tea.

Tea caddies of bygone years have become highly collectable as pieces of art and design because no two are the same. This causes me to think of our great Creator who has made each one of us unique and we are most precious to Him. If we allow Him, He wants to place within us His precious treasure, His very own nature, so we can be a blessing to our fellowman.

Today quite large and ornate tea caddies are mostly found in hotels, although I have seen them in some private houses. These do not hold loose tea but rather a variety of herbal teas in the form of tea bags and a few tea bags of regular tea. I do have a complaint about this arrangement. Whenever invited to select a tea from the caddy I choose the "proper" tea bag, of course! Always, when drinking the tea, I would detect the flavor from the herbal tea bags, which had penetrated the regular tea bag. This is quite unacceptable to me; I guess my taste buds are very sensitive where tea is concerned.

In this day and age there is no need to lock up tea caddies, but they must be perfectly airtight and kept in a cool place. Modern caddies are usually made of metal and can be quite attractive, but do not have the sheer beauty and character of the original caddies which reflected the value of the contents. Sometimes I have seen people use tea straight from an opened packet, with little regard to the flavor which is being lost by being exposed to the air.

We must take heed that we do not neglect or take for granted the precious endowment we have received from our Great Creator, but to present our bodies as a living sacrifice, holy, acceptable to God, which is our reasonable service. (Romans 12:1) We need to guard and protect that which God has given us.

# Chapter 5

## England Captivated by Tea

It is hard to imagine the first shipments of tea to England only weighed from as little as 7 lbs. The scarcity, of course, increased its value, I would think on a par with diamonds! Tea was only to be found in the possession of the highest in the land. In time the taste for tea began to spread to more and more people of the aristocracy.

To transport tea quickly special three-masted ships called "Clippers" were constructed. They would compete with each other to see how quickly they could complete the journey from China to England with the precious cargo. I fancy the name "Clipper" was given because they would see how much time could be "clipped" off a journey. The competition inspired feverish wagers as to who would be first to sail up the River Thames and so receive the best price for the cargo.

When one thinks of clipper sailing ships, immediately comes to mind the well known "Cutty Sark", which I understand was the most frequent record breaker for speed. The Cutty Sark's final resting place is in the London Docks where a fire occurred recently and unfortunately the ship was damaged, but happily, restoration is to take place. Thus it will be possible to see how tea was transported in days gone by.

Very soon more and more tea was imported into the country and the government saw this as a means of increasing revenues. A huge tax was put on the importation of tea, driving the prices sky high. Despite the astronomically high price, the demand for tea increased in every strata of English society.

Many were the devious ways of obtaining the delectable tea. Maidservants of the aristocracy would make tea for themselves from the once brewed tea then sell the twice brewed tea at the back door. Such was the desire for what was once described as the "democratic herb".

There are, and always have been rascally traders around, so it is not surprising to learn that such people discovered ways to undercut the very highly priced tea. This was done by mixing tea with ash leaves boiled in iron sulfate and sheep's dung. This was nicknamed "smooch".

The southern rugged coastline of England was suitable for smugglers to bring to shore such high priced commodities as tea. On a very dark night, it would be smuggled from ships on to small boats, a horse and cart would be at the ready. The horse's hooves would be covered with rags to muffle the clip-clop as they made their way to the next stop.

No one had any qualms about purchasing smuggled tea; certainly there would be an extremely heavy punishment if one was found out. Even coastal clergy would allow their crypts to be used by the smugglers. Records show that one, Parson Woodforde, wrote "Andrew the Smuggler brought me this night about eleven o'clock a bag of Hyson Tea, 6lbs weight. He frightened us by whistling under the parlor window just as we were going to bed."

For once, the rich people were unable to keep the best things to themselves. At this time two pleasure gardens in Vauxhall, London began to make tea available to the general public. For a small price you could gain admittance and if you so desired, avail yourself of the delicious beverage, tea. It would be quite a common occurrence for a lady of noble birth to be elbow to elbow with a serving maid as they meandered around the lantern lit gardens.

It was in such a setting that the abbreviation T.I.P.S. came into being. There could be a considerably long time to wait before one was served tea so this could be overcome by presenting T.I.P.S. before being served. T.I.P.S. simply means, "to insure prompt service". So the original tip came before, not after being served!

The passion for tea spread to the very lowly working people; people, who in fact were called peasants and were despised by the upper classes. Their breakfast consisted of gin and whatever food was available. The gin was very cheap, so much so that it was said "drunk for a penny, dead drunk for two pennies".

There was a certain high ranking man by the name of William Cobbett, who was infuriated that the average laborer spent one third of his earnings on tea and thus denounced tea as a wicked waste of time and money. He went on to say that it rendered the frame feeble, thus creating a softness and effeminacy and caused the laborers to become idle. In fact, tea had just the opposite effect; people were healthier on account of the water being boiled to make tea. Also common sense tells you that drinking huge quantities of gin every day is the quickest way to shorten life. Tea was the star beverage at temperance meetings of the 1830s and often the tea urn was manned by a reformed drunkard for maximum moral effect.

Very soon, what are now known as "Tea Shops" began to flourish everywhere. Of course there was no charge to go into such places and this made them very popular with ordinary people. Tea-cakes or other desirable delicacies could be served with your tea or you could just drink tea.

Waitresses usually wore black dresses, pretty lace caps and aprons and black shoes. They were nicknamed "nippies". I think possibly this was for two reasons; they were adept at moving quickly between tables and usually were of a very cheerful disposition. Being served by such cheerful young ladies only increased the pleasure of taking tea. You can go anywhere in England today and still find this cheerful atmosphere pervading tea rooms.

By the year 1826 an honest Quaker, by the name of John Horniman, had the idea of measuring tea into sealed packages. This was an excellent idea as it put an end to smooch, as each packet of tea was of a guaranteed weight and quality. I well remember the brand, Horniman's Tea, when I was a child. Eventually Horniman was bought out by two orphaned teenage brothers, the Tetleys, who began their career pedaling tea to the almost inaccessible Yorkshire Dales.

I see a parallel between the irresistible urge of people of every class to drink tea and the people who hear the Good News of the Gospel of the Lord Jesus Christ. For countless numbers of people of every class, who hear of God's love, are touched in such a way that they find it irresistible. To be touched by the love of God is to have a consuming passion for God and just nothing can ever erase it. Today we can purchase tea at a relatively low cost, but as I have explained this was not always so. In like manner, the freedom we enjoy today to worship God and teach His ways through His Word, was brought to us in bygone days by the courage of many, who paid the ultimate price, some being burned at the stake. This should cause us to value and prize more highly that which we enjoy today.

# Chapter 6

## Tea comes to America

I have reason to believe that tea reached America before it was accepted in England as at this time there was no opposition to tea, in fact it was greatly enjoyed by the English settlers. These settlers were under the Crown and the British were always quick to find ways of increasing revenues by introducing stamp duty and other similar methods to finance war efforts.

The British Government became aware of the American Colonists' great love for tea and decided to exploit this by placing a tax on tea exported to America. We all know the early settlers were made of very stern stuff, having already made the decision to leave England rather than violate their consciences with regard to their personal beliefs.

As stated previously, the British Government had already placed a huge tax on tea sold in Britain and this resulted in a massive accumulation of tea in the warehouses of the British East India Company. Most people were getting their tea by devious means.

Now that colonists had a great love for tea, the British Government gave permission for the East India Company to export tea to America, selling direct to retailers, thus cutting out the middle man, while at the same time greatly increasing the coffers of the British Government. This situation angered the merchants of the colonies to such an extent that John Hancock organized a boycott of tea from China. Matters worsened when the British Government decided to impose a massive tax on tea. There was resentment coming from every quarter and finally it came to the boil with the "Boston Tea Party". A number of men disguised as

Mohawk Indians boarded the ship, Dartmouth, to unload its cargo. They certainly unloaded it; the forty-five tons of tea were unloaded into the sea! As one would expect, punitive measures were taken by the British, resulting in the closure of the port of Boston.

From that time on the colonists boycotted tea, even though the women loved the beverage they were willing to support the boycott. This event became significant in the build up to the War of Independence. In view of all this, William Pitt, the British Prime Minister obtained a repeal of the tax, but of course, the damage was already done. However, there still remained a few people who did not stifle their love of tea. As I understand, one such was General George Washington, no less, who was never without his cup of tea even when on army maneuvers.

Many years later during the World Fair Exhibition in St Louis an enterprising man thought to sell tea to the many visitors. Unfortunately the weather was exceedingly hot and humid so no one showed any interest in sampling piping hot tea. He was not about to give up easily, so he came up with the idea of cooling the tea with ice. Lo and behold, he was on to a winner; the crowds flocked to sample this amazing iced drink so 'Iced Tea' was birthed in the U.S.A. It has remained a very popular drink especially in the summer months. Almost everyone I know in the U.S.A. drinks iced tea, yet relatively few of my friends drink hot tea. This seems a mystery to me.

It was an American who invented tea bags. These were readily adopted in America but struggled to be accepted by the British. The 'Brits' had the idea that tea bags were made up of sweepings from loose tea. I will write about this in more detail in a later chapter.

During these last few years there has been a great surge of interest in afternoon or high teas. Establishments have sprung up all over the country and many hotels have rooms set aside to create the correct ambience for such occasions. Since living in the U.S.A. I have been to many American afternoon teas in hotels, tea shops, at private functions and once in the National Cathedral. On the whole I have been favorably impressed, with just one disappointing hotel experience. (I am sure they did what they thought to be their best, but I do not wish to say any more about it.)

One of my very best tea experiences was when my friend took me to the Watergate Hotel. The whole incident exceeded my wildest dreams as the experience was an utter delight, leaving nothing else to be desired. They just had it all! I will be writing later about the finer details of afternoon tea but I wish to mention one thing I had never seen before. Of course, one doesn't pour one's own tea; that is done by the hostess or if you are having tea out, it is done by the waitress. Our waitress poured out our tea through a strainer. This strainer was different, because when the tea was poured the waitress released a gadget which covered the under part of the strainer, thus eliminating the possibility of drops of tea being dripped. I thought this was 'real neat'.

It's a funny thing, but just when you think you have seen it all, something else comes along to fill you with surprise and delight.

Easter 2008, my friend took me along with her to Beaufort, S.C. On the whole I was struck by the tranquility and friendship of the people. A good example of this was shown on the day we went out to the tea house called "a lil-bit o' heaven". On arriving I couldn't help but catch my breath. It was a small cottage set in a quiet rural setting. The wisteria and azaleas were in full bloom. Planters filled with flowers adorned the steps and patio. Welcoming signs were posted all over.

Inside was just an extension of what was outside. There were only two small cozy tea rooms which exuded warmth and ambience. The walls were liberally decorated with highly colorful hats and we were invited to choose one to wear as we had tea. Here and there were plaques with uplifting messages on them and all these good things were even in the restrooms. There was no rush or bustle as we were waited on by the proprietors' daughter, who was demurely dressed in a long black dress and wearing a lovely hat.

We were served in a very sweet and leisurely manner, just as if we had all the time in the world. All the dainty food was hand-made on the premises, and yes, I can say it was all authentically English in its whole presentation. The place certainly deserved and lived up to its name "a lil-bit o' heaven". Should you ever be in the area of S.C. please do yourself a favor and take time to have tea in this most delightful tea room.

So, tea is still alive and well in America, in fact, its popularity is increasing. This causes me to think of God's Word, even though at times there have been attempts to quell it, yet it ever remains strong and cannot be resisted, but has a deep lodging place in the hearts and lives of thousands of people world-wide.

*Dolly and friends take tea at "a lil-bit-o-heaven"*

# Chapter 7

## I am reluctant to say

Yes, this is a chapter I would like to omit, but the story needs to be recorded even though it will be a somewhat shortened version.

All of this occurred between the years 1834 and 1842. At the same time, China was demanding silver for the exchange of tea. England was already off the gold standard so sought other means to find the required revenue. At this time, India was under the control of England. Cotton was the main crop in India and provided people with their livelihood. With the full consent of the government, the East Indian Trading Company began to cultivate poppies for opium, almost decimating the cotton industry.

The idea was to export opium to China and with this revenue, be able to pay for large quantities of tea for England. As tea was still a very expensive commodity, it brought huge profits into the national treasury. It did not take long before China became addicted to smoking opium with devastating effects on the health of its people. I may add that opium had been widely used in many countries for years but only for medicinal purposes. This state of affairs was not going to be tolerated by the Chinese Government. A law was passed banning the import of opium. For a while, this law had little effect; for one thing, the opium was imported into the ports of Southern China and the seat of government was in Northern China. There was an enormous amount of money exchanged buying and selling opium.

At one point, the Chinese Government made an appeal to Queen Victoria to intervene and end the export of opium from India to China. There was less than an enthusiastic response because it is reported that the Queen was not averse to smoking opium herself. It has to be said the British Government was also aware of the proposal to ban opium exports to China, but preferred to turn a blind eye and receive the enormous revenue it created.

There were attempts to put an end to the opium traffic and minor skirmishes ensued at sea by the use of the Chinese military. The situation became critical when the son of the reigning Emperor died as a result of taking opium. The Emperor applied rigorous force to end the import of opium. There was one occasion when the Emperor's troops succeeded in throwing a vast amount of opium into the sea. This aroused the fury of the East Indian Trading Company as they witnessed the demise of a great amount of revenue. Great Britain's response was to retaliate by bringing in the great guns, which almost devastated many of the southern ports of China, killing great numbers of innocent civilians. China was no match for this kind of onslaught so was compelled to sign an agreement to give several ports, including Hong Kong, to England. So the opium trade continued because there were plenty of Chinese traders willing to contravene the law by smuggling the banned opium into the country.

The beautiful flowers of the Camelia Sinensus and the poppy were created for the benefit and not the destruction of mankind; they had been violated to satisfy man's lust for money. Looking back into the pages of history it can also be said that the beautiful message of the gospel has also been violated in a way God never intended, bringing hatred and mistrust in its train. Despite all that has happened in the past, tea is still drunk and enjoyed by millions of people the world over. Likewise, the power of the gospel is still transforming the lives of thousands of people and it is from those individuals we can truly see what the message of Christianity is all about.

The story of tea now takes another turn, and this time for the better. First, tea had been found to be growing in the mountainous regions of India, which were much closer to England. Secondly, the days of the sailing ships were drawing to a close with the introduction of steam ships, which traveled much faster and were more reliable than sailing vessels. Thirdly, the great engineering feat of the Suez Canal connecting the Red Sea to the Mediterranean reduced the journey considerably.

Having suffered through this unpleasant chapter, I gladly move on to the more pleasant side of the tea story; so now we will move forward with anticipation of good things!

# Chapter 8

## Teapots, cups, saucers and more

To enhance the pleasure of drinking tea, artisans introduced a great variety of beautiful things to be used whenever tea was being taken. For quite a while teapots and cups and saucers were made from earthenware. Teapots were so made to have holes just where the spout began. This was so that tea could be poured whilst leaving most of the tea leaves behind.

We all seem to be born with a sense of appreciating beauty and it wasn't long before this expressed itself in the beautifying of everything to do with tea. In the 18th century in Staffordshire England, there lived the Wedgwood family, who were famous for the production of earthenware.

Josiah Wedgwood was the youngest of a very large family. As a result of getting smallpox as a child, he was unable to work the potter's wheel because he was so badly crippled in his left leg. His creativity began to express itself in his experimenting with pottery. He invented lovely glazes and colors and created attractive designs which had a tremendous appeal to lovers of tea. Josiah would always have his wife test each teapot to make sure it poured out correctly. It is said that he smashed anything which did not meet his high standard.

One of the patrons was Queen Charlotte, who loved the cream ware he produced. In her honor it was named "Queens Ware" and it is still popular today. At this time the price of Wedgwood porcelain was within the reach of most people, except for the poorest of the poor.

By now the marketing for everything to do with tea drinking was in full swing. Gradually the market moved into producing fine porcelain and bone china. This was so fine and delicate you could see your fingers through it, yet it had the advantage of keeping the tea very hot. There are many famous names in the china industry and they have been around for a considerable time. Some of these are Minton, Derby, Worcester, Royal Dalton and Royal Albert. The shapes, designs and patterns of these alter over the years, but many are extremely beautiful and must give great delight to their users. This kind of tea ware is expensive and is not something one may wish to use everyday. Often this china becomes an heirloom to be passed on from generation to generation. A cheaper variety of china can be bought which can be beautifully decorated but does not have the hallmark of the prestigious names already mentioned.

An incident comes to my mind which happened to me many years ago. I was visiting a lady who had the reputation of being the richest lady for many miles around. It was summer-time and she decided we could take tea in the garden. She served the tea in her Royal Derby teacups. I was in total agony in case I should have a mishap with this precious china. I had never before drunk from such fragile valuable china and I have never done since.

I guess I have seen hundreds of teapots in my life time. Let me tell you of one which, for me, distinguishes it from all the others.

I saw this amazing teapot at a ladies' afternoon tea function. At first sight there was nothing of outstanding beauty; it was blue and white and fairly long in shape. You could also add as a bonus, it was made by Josiah Wedgwood. Now, what was it that made it so special to me? Let me tell you.

On both sides of the teapot were some lines of poetry written. These are the words:

Be present at our table, Lord.
Be here and everywhere adored.
Thy creatures bless and grant that we
May feast in Paradise with Thee.


We thank Thee, Lord, for this our food,
But more because of Jesus' blood.
Let manna to our souls be given.
The bread of life sent down from heaven.

The reproduction of this teapot was of the original, which had been given by Josiah Wedgwood to Hannah Wesley who, as you will recall, was the wife of Charles Wesley. The sight of this teapot flooded me with memories from my school days. In those days children always went home mid-day for lunch and before we were dismissed, we had to stand and sing the first verse of the same words which adorned the Hannah Wesley teapot. On our return from lunch, as we were assembled for afternoon lessons, again we all had to stand and sing the words found on the reverse side of the teapot. We sang them to the tune Doxology.

In England the most popular tea service is "Old Country Rose" by the makers of Royal Albert. The reason for its popularity is that way back in the 1950s a weekly television show was being shown called "The Forsythe Saga". This story was set in the Victorian era and it was "Old Country Rose" china which was always used as the cast were taking tea. Old Country Rose is still being produced today owing to popular demand. It is not only available as a tea service, but as a dinner service and a great number of other items as well. The best thing about it is that should any get broken they can easily be replaced.

In Victorian times most of the men grew fairly large moustaches. Someone introduced the idea of creating a cup with a ledge inside to prevent a moustache dipping into the tea; thus it was called a "mustachio cup". As time passed there was a small departure from regular shaped cups. Tea was usually served with a cup and saucer, the saucer useful for catching spills from an overfull teacup, as well as being a suitable resting place for the accompanying teaspoon. Sometimes the saucer was used to tuck in a biscuit or two, as it was customary in England to offer biscuits with tea.

As tea drinking became so popular, breakages of cups and saucers were inevitable, especially when cups were placed in the hands of young children. Some enterprising person had the idea to produce enamel mugs. I remember as a child we were not allowed to drink out of regular cups but we each had an enamel cup. I may add, besides the mug, we each had an enamel plate. In time these became chipped, but we still had to use them, "chipped an' all".

In time mugs made of porcelain etc. began to flood the market. They would hold around half a pint of tea so you can see the practicality of such an idea for a tea loving nation. They are easy on the eye and very comforting to hold. Originally one would never dream of offering guests a mug to drink from and certainly they would not appear on the table which was laid out for a meal.

Time certainly changes things, and sure enough, people became bold enough to offer guests tea in a mug. In fact, when offered the choice of a cup or a mug, 99% of the time the answer would be "a mug". It seems that lovely china cups and saucers are only brought out on very special occasions or when people are presenting tea in the "oldie world way".

Things have departed even further from the original cup of tea in delicate china cups with the invention of paper cups. Some would say they are hygienic and convenient, especially as they do not require washing. I have to confess that paper teacups are one of my pet hates and I avoid them whenever possible. Certainly, if it meant not having tea because there were no china cups available, I would make the best of it, just to savor the stimulating refreshing tea.

All I have recorded about the variety of teapots and teacups causes me to realize the most important thing which really matters is the authenticity of the contents of them, namely tea! I learn from all this, the very important truth of God's Word which states, "we have this treasure in earthen vessels." The treasure is the very life of God through Jesus Christ dwelling within those who receive Him. Cups were designed to contain tea; we were designed to contain God's gift of eternal life through Jesus, His Son. The neat thing is that God does not choose us for our outward appearance, however good that may be, or discard us for our less than good appearance. But God Almighty is longing to invade the life of anyone who will receive Him. With the receiving, there comes a pouring out to others that they too may be filled with "authentic" tea. I am sure you can see the analogy I am trying to make.

*Dolly's friend Ethel serving tea from Old Country Rose China*

# Chapter 9

## At last P.E.T.

Now is the time to get down to the P.E.T. yes, P.E.T. meaning "perfect English tea". I would like to make it quite clear that I am not laying down any laws dictating how anyone should make tea. I am about to explain to you the way to make tea the English way. The only absolute requirement for making tea by any method which suits you is to make sure you have authentic tea which comes from the tree, Camellia Sinensis.

Tea is grown in the regions of India, Sri Lanka, Kenya and of course China. All these teas are black. We have Darjeeling from India, which has a slightly astringent flavor. Assam from India is full-bodied with a rich smooth malty flavor. We have Ceylon Blend from Sri Lanka which is brisk, full of flavor with a bright color. Then there is Kenya tea which is a strong tea with a brisk flavor. All these teas can be taken with or without milk. Whichever tea you choose depends on your taste. Manufacturers usually produce their own particular blend by combining several of the teas mentioned.

There are a host of good names from which to choose, such as Taylors of Yorkshire, Yorkshire, Yorkshire Gold, P.G. Tips, Typhoo Tea, Tetleys Tea, Harrods, just to mention a few of the very best. I will deal with Earl Grey tea a little later, but for now I will proceed with the all important P.E.T.

Fill your kettle with freshly drawn water. Put it on the stove to bring it up to the boil. Have ready your teapot and rinse it out with very hot water. Add to the teapot one teaspoon or one tea bag for each cup to be served. This amount may vary according to your personal taste. This is a good guide, but if your tea is too strong you can always add more hot water. The next step is all important and crucial to making the P.E.T.

Watch the kettle carefully as it is nearing boiling point. Have your teapot close at hand and immediately the water comes to a rolling boil pour it over the tea and put on the lid and cover the teapot with a tea cozy. You may wonder why the haste to get the boiling water to the pot. The boiling water contains oxygen and this is crucial to bring out the full flavor of the tea. Let the tea stand for three to five minutes.

At one time tea was always sold in leaf form. Later on came the tea bag. Does it really matter, you may be asking. Well, that all depends on the sensitivity of your taste buds.

Let's take a peep inside the pot whose tea is made from what is termed as "loose leaf tea". I should add here that leaves of the very best teas are usually larger than the less expensive teas and so will take a little longer to brew. As soon as the boiling water hits the dried tea leaves in the pot it causes them to unfurl gradually, releasing all the long pent up fragrance and flavor from where it originated; could be the mountains of Kenya or Sri Lanka, who knows.

I have to break off here to tell you how much this all reminds me of God's own Son who left Heaven, so far away, and He was willing to allow Himself to have God's wrath poured upon Him on the cross so that we could be free and able to drink new life from His sacrifice for us. Yes, as the tea leaves unfurl and yield to boiling water, that's how Jesus yielded Himself to the cross for us so that we may drink freely of all His life means.

There are some minor facts associated with the P.E.T. experience. Originally tea was taken without anything added to it. However, it is perfectly acceptable to add sugar if desired. Honey would not be acceptable, but if you prefer honey, go right ahead. It is correct to add regular milk according to your taste. It is not customary to use cream or instant milk but if you want to do so, then again, go right ahead.

I have come to recognize that not everyone conforms to the accepted P.E.T. Here are some examples. A while ago an Indian gentleman visited my granddaughter's home where I was living at the time. I thought I would like to please him by making him a P.E.T. He was less than impressed and began forthwith to make tea the Indian way. This was done by boiling tea and sugar in the teapot for a long time until it became a black syrupy substance.

I was already feeling somewhat offended by his disdain of what I regarded as the ultimate P.E.T., so when he offered me a taste of his special brew I felt a little reluctant to accept. I am glad that my better self emerged and I did take a sip. I found it altogether repugnant, but I came to realize that for him, that was the perfect cup of tea.

Long ago, I had a friend in England who drank her tea made entirely of hot water with barely a teaspoonful of tea poured into her cup. The color was the palest of straw color you could get. She had lots of sugar with it and no milk. I think I was the only person whom could fix it to her liking.

I think this next example is quite amusing. Our friend Dan always adds ice cubes to his tea. As I see it, one of the hallmarks of a good cup of tea is to drink it piping hot. I will give one more illustration.

My friend Donald, in England, passionately loves Earl Grey tea. (I will be writing more about Earl Grey tea later.) Donald has the idea that because he loves Earl Grey tea everyone else should share his passion. When I was visiting their home for a while, Donald tried his utmost to persuade me to drink his favorite tea. It so happens that I heartily dislike Earl Grey so his chances of persuading me were nil.

One day, as I was drinking tea which Donald had made, I was detecting an unfamiliar taste in the tea. At first, I thought, maybe the tea was stale, which can happen if the tea has not been stored in an airtight container. I really did not like to say anything, so I tried to take just the tiniest of sips. Finally, I couldn't keep up the façade any longer so I said to Donald, "Donald, I think this tea has a peculiar taste." At that he broke out laughing. By adding a small quantity of Earl Grey to the regular tea he had thought to trick me into drinking it, and then he could say I had drunk Earl Grey and didn't know the difference. I think I finally convinced him of my dislike of Earl Grey.

One thing is very clear; tea is present throughout all the incidents I have just recalled. A valuable lesson can be learned from all of this. Sometimes Christians try to impose their own style of worship on others. We need to realize that different people worship God in different ways. So long as we worship the one and only true God, as He is shown in the face of Jesus Christ, it is not important how we worship, but it is important whom we worship. We do well to heed the words of Jesus when He said, "They that worship me must worship in spirit and in truth, the Lord seeketh such to worship Him". John 4: 23

# Chapter 10

## More Tales from the Teapot

We have a saying in England which goes like this, "the second cup of tea never tastes like the first one". I can assure you this is a very true statement. I never ever knew or even thought to understand the reason why and never, for that matter, did anyone else I knew. Everything does have a reason why and it so happened that a short time ago I discovered the reason why. After the tea has fully brewed, if not poured out right away, the tea begins to release the caffeine which resides in the leaves, thus causing the different taste in the second cup of tea.

There are ways to avoid this. The simplest way is to make just enough tea to fill each cup, then rinse out the teapot and begin again. If you are using loose tea you could fill a "tea-ball" with the dried tea and place it in the warmed teapot, removing it when the tea has brewed. By doing this the second cup should taste as good as the first. If using tea bags, the method is the same; it is very easy to scoop the tea bags from the teapot and dispose of them.

It seems strange, but as far back as 1669 there were some people who had learned the secret of keeping tea fresh. I wish to quote one such person, who was described as "the Eminently Learned Sir Kenlemn Digby Knight".

"In these parts....... we let the hot water remain too long soaking upon the tea, which makes its extract into itself the earthy part of the herb. The water is to remain upon it, no longer than whiles you can say the Miserere Psalm very leisurely..... Thus you have only the spiritual parts of the tea, which is much more active, penetrating and friendly to mature."

Let me also give you another noteworthy quotation from 1750 entitled, "A treatise on the inherent qualities of the Tea-Herb" compiled by a Gentleman of Cambridge. "Your tea-leaf tho' never so good when you buy, will lose itself, being of a very volatile spirit, unless carefully preserved in silver, pewter, or tin boxes, shut close from the air; and above all, kept from the damps and neighbourhood of strong scents, sweet or offensive."

Another quote is from the middle of the 18th century. Dr Johnson was an early addict to tea and described himself as a "hardened and shameless tea drinker, who has for twenty years diluted his meals with only the infusion of this fascinating plant; whose kettle has scarcely time to cool; who with tea amuses the evening, with tea solaces the midnight, and with tea welcomes the morning."

A quote from De-Quincy, a notable from bygone years goes thus: "Tea, though ridiculed by those who are naturally course in their nervous sensibilities, or are become so from wine-drinking, and are not susceptible to influence from so refined a stimulant, will always be the favoured beverage of the intellectual."

# Chapter 11

## Girls Love Tea-time

In England almost every girl will have a porcelain miniature tea-set among her favorite playthings. I remember, as a child, enjoying hours of pleasure pretending to be grown-up as I played with sisters and friends at tea parties. It really was pretend because we only had imaginary tea, sugar and milk.

I have had many fun times having tea with my great granddaughters and even my great grandsons enjoy drinking tea. There have been occasions when my great granddaughters would dress up in my fancy hats, scarves, purses and gloves to enjoy drinking tea. At those times they were allowed to use the best Old Country Rose china. It was such fun watching them holding their cups in a dainty fashion with fingers outspread, as they had seen in films. They would make quite a ritual of it.

A few years ago I had put on an English tea as part of a fundraiser for a worthy cause. There were one or two young girls who came and everyone was suitably dressed for the occasion. I guess for these girls it was their first English tea. This was evident from what one girl did. She proceeded to put milk in her tea, and then upon seeing others put lemon juice in their tea, thought the proper way was for her to add lemon juice to hers. You can guess the result, a cup full of curdled tea. I am glad I noticed what was going on and so I explained to her that you put either milk or lemon in tea, never both. It was a mistake any child could make, but I am certain she would never do that again.

There was a time when my granddaughter Lois and her friend Heather decided they would like to plunge in and explore the mystery of taking afternoon tea. They had the house to themselves and I happened to arrive as they were experimenting. They had taken the best china out of the cupboard and were having a glorious time together. There was laughter and giggling as they were balancing their teacups and saucers in what they perceived as a most ladylike manner. I tell you, I had a lot of fun watching the whole process. To this day, Lois still loves a cup of tea.

I do hope that little girls will continue to dress up and enjoy taking tea in an elegant fashion; it really is a delightful feminine thing to do.

*Dolly's great granddaughters Olivia and Octavia
are ready for tea*

# Chapter 12

## Of Lord Sandwich and Earl Grey

It would be unthinkable to write a book about tea and not include these two worthy gentlemen, to whom we owe so much for the fascinating history of English tea-time. Afternoon tea should start with sandwiches of various fillings. The first sandwich dates back to the year 1762. Like many things, 'necessity is the mother of invention' and this was so true of the very first sandwich.

The Earl of Sandwich was known for the daredevil kind of life he used to live. He had a reputation for being a gambler, hurling his fortunes around from gaming table to gaming table. Often his gambling sessions would last twenty-four hours or more. It was on one of these nights that the rumblings of his empty stomach were distracting him from the combinations of clubs and diamonds. He had a very good hand and did not wish to rise for a meal exclaiming, "Stap me vitals!" I guess you can easily interpret what he meant.

Suddenly a great inspiration came to him. Whispering to his manservant, he gave him the order to go down to the kitchen and fix him a hunk of beef between two slices of bread. The gamblers all gasped in admiration at such brilliance and so the very first sandwich was invented. I may add that Lord Sandwich went on to win 10 thousand pounds that night, which I am sure in our present day values would be equivalent to one million dollars.

We would have a difficult time today imagining life without a sandwich. Probably someone else would have had the same idea but it would not have been called "sandwich". There is no end to the variety of sandwiches being served nowadays, but I think nothing could be more satisfying to a hungry man than an Angus beef sandwich taken with a large mug of very hot, sweet, strong tea.

The Earl Grey story, very different from the Earl of Sandwich story, has its origins in China. It is so named after the second Earl Grey, who was the Prime Minister during the reign of William IV in 1830.

One of Earl Grey's envoys was on a diplomatic trip to China. I do not have the full facts of what happened exactly, but what I do know is that the envoy saved the life of a wealthy mandarin. The Chinese are known for being very gracious and the mandarin responded in true Chinese fashion. The mandarin expressed his gratitude to the envoy by sending Earl Grey a delicate blend of scented tea. The blend consisted of large leafed Darjeeling China tea with the addition of oil of bergamot. This oil is obtained from the pear shaped citrus fruit of the bergamot shrub. It gives a fragrant flavor to the tea and is especially good to take with cakes and sweet things.

So, from the heroic deed of the envoy we have this universally loved tea. Ironically, this gift was given to Earl Grey, who had nothing to do with the deed of valor performed by his envoy. Sometimes life is like that, others get the praise for something we have done. Obviously the tea was very well appreciated and from that time it became known as Earl Grey Tea. In those days this tea was not considered a lowly gift as only the wealthy could afford to buy tea. I imagine it would have been heavily guarded similar to the way we guard our jewelry today. It was regarded as a tea drunk only by those of high social status.

When I was a child, occasionally I would hear people refer to Earl Grey Tea with a sense of awe. I did not know of anyone who actually drank it, nor did I see it on sale in my local grocery stores. I guess it could only be purchased from such illustrious stores as Harrods. Things have certainly changed now. It all began slowly, the emergence of Earl Grey Tea in regular stores.

In England some people like to "take on airs and graces", much like Mrs Buquet in the television show, "Keeping up appearances". With the introduction of Earl Grey some people loved to admit they bought the tea as if it made them "a cut above everyone else". We human beings are so funny and that is what makes us endearing to the heart of God.

Nowadays, every store sells Earl Grey and a recent addition is Lady Grey. There are distinct characteristics about Earl Grey. Although it is a black tea from Darjeeling, when brewed it is always a light brown color. No matter how much tea you use, it will never turn any darker. Earl Grey is not taken with milk or cream, although you may add sugar or lemon juice. Traditionally it is taken at tea-time, around 4 p.m. although this is no reason for you to adhere to such custom

From what I have already mentioned in an earlier chapter you will know that I have an aversion to Earl Grey, but I have tried to write in a non-prejudicial way, and I truly hope you will continue to enjoy this very British tea with such a fascinating story linked to it.

# Chapter 13

## The Ritz Experience

No book about tea would be complete without the elegant story of tea at the Ritz. I must confess I have yet to have the personal pleasure of taking tea at the Ritz, but it is not too late. I am sure that one day it will be my pleasurable surprise to do so. Meanwhile, my imagination is fired from the knowledge I have gained from different sources.

In my much younger days the term "putting on the Ritz" was often quoted, indicating that all the stops were pulled out to ensure a good time was had by all. Now I have really discovered what "putting on the Ritz" really means.

In Switzerland in the year 1850 Caesar Ritz was born He came from a farming family, which was not surprising, coming from Switzerland. From an early age he had an interest in culinary delights and so he went on to work in several hotels, no doubt gaining much experience and insight.

In 1898, with his partner Georges Auguste Escoffier, he opened a hotel in Paris which he named "The Ritz". From its beginning the Ritz was known both far and wide for its elegance and warmth. The list of people of great renown, who have enjoyed and are still enjoying the unique ambience of the place, is endless. Some have even spent their last days there, finding the peace and tranquility they desired. Also it has been the setting for numerous films, movies and plays.

The London Ritz was opened on May 24th 1906 and obviously designed with a French theme in the style of Louis XVI. The hotel itself is flanked with marble pillars, quiet alcoves, gilded arches and of course, elegant furniture and carpeting. Fresh flowers are a feature and playful fountains pour forth from graceful nymphs.

It was around this time that the craze for drinking tea was increasing significantly. The idea was birthed in Caesar Ritz's mind to create a tea-room within his hotel. The setting for this was to be the Palm Court, separated from the main gallery by Ionic columns. It seems that Ritz intended people to enter a world of exquisite beauty, tranquility and harmony, where time did not exist, this being achieved by the absence of clocks.

The color scheme was mainly rose pink and these included chairs, tables and the pink-capped chandeliers. Ritz went to great lengths to produce the kind of lighting which would make people appear more beautiful than they were. He knew this would enhance their enjoyment of having tea. It took hours and hours of experimenting with various colors before any decision was made. Ritz's wife had to sit during these hours whilst the electrician tried different colored lighting and eventually it was agreed that apricot-pink was the most becoming color. How thoughtful to go to such lengths.

The appeal of "Tea at the Ritz" caused some people to stand around waiting for a vacant table and this disturbed Ritz somewhat. Rather than regarding this as evidence of a profitable business, he considered it more a detraction from the tranquil atmosphere he had sought to create. He solved this problem by making it possible for people to make reservations in advance.

People were required to arrive suitably dressed, collar and tie for men and dresses or dress suits for women. Part of the pleasure of taking tea at the Ritz was viewing the beautiful hats, fans and dresses worn by the ladies. Should it ever happen that a thoughtless person arrived for tea, unsuitably attired, they would be very courteously but firmly escorted from the premises.

I am not sure how many Ritz Hotels there are; I do know of the ones in Paris, London and Washington D.C. Maybe there are others, but one thing can be said, Ritz has set such a high standard, many other hotels have tried to emulate. As the years roll by, there is still an irresistible fascination with the Ritz style of taking tea. I have noticed that people, especially ladies, enjoy dressing up for the occasion. This is refreshing, as nowadays the general fashion trend seems to be as casual as possible. If you dress regularly in a rather formal way some may consider you rather odd.

How could I possibly write about the achievement of Caesar Ritz without being reminded of the comforting words of Jesus to His disciples, just before He left this world, "I go to prepare a place for you"? It was our Creator who endowed Ritz with the creativity to create the Ritz tea experience. How much more will the Creator create a place in Heaven for each one of us, which will far exceed our imagination? That place will be a place of perfect harmony and beauty. The best part is that God Himself will provide suitable garments to wear, garments not of our own choosing, but we will be clothed with garments of righteousness, which have been paid for in full, through the death of God's own Son, Jesus.

# Chapter 14

## Time for Tea

There is only one correct time to take tea, that would be any time between midnight and midnight the following day! In other words, there is never a time when it is inappropriate to delight one's heart in the enjoyment of drinking tea. Disraeli made the claim that he drank more tea between the hours of midnight and dawn than any other subject.

The amount of tea drunk by individuals varies according to taste, but probably it would be safe to say that on average it could be about 2 ½ cups a day. Of course there are complete abstainers in England; maybe that comes as a surprise to you. On the other hand there are the excessive tea drinkers. I knew of one such excessive tea drinker. He was my son's father-in-law, Dave. Whenever I was in Dave's company he was never separated from his mug of tea. Whenever he and his wife were visiting us for a while, I always made sure he had plenty of tea on hand.

One day, for a bit of fun, I said to him, "Dave, can I get you a cup of tea?" His predictable answer, spoken in his London accent was, "I thought you would never 'arsk'". This gave rise to a lot of laughter at his sense of humor because it was only thirty minutes since I had served him tea.

I guess most people are familiar with the phrase, "English Breakfast Tea". I have no idea where this phrase came from, because English Breakfast Tea can be drunk at any time of the day and possesses the same high quality flavor as any other good tea. Maybe the name itself gives the idea of something very bracing, because it has to be admitted that many of us feel like a bracing beverage at breakfast time. Whenever I am offered a varied selection of tea bags I would always choose the English Breakfast, knowing I would be getting *authentic* English tea.

## "A welcome cuppa"

"How about a cuppa tea, luv?" was the voice I heard as I was lying in a semi-conscious state in Macclesfield General Hospital. The voice had a distinct northern English accent, the sound of it pulling me back to a conscious frame of mind. Eyes widened at the wholesome picture before me. Here he came, a senior citizen with an obvious disability, trundling a tea-trolley, offering cups of refreshing tea to willing recipients.

He approached my bed with the same cheerfulness he had extended to others. There was no elegance, china teacups or lacy tablecloths, but the manner in which this senior citizen presented a cup of tea invoked in me a sense of warmth and empathy. Here was that special touch which helps bring healing.

I do not know the name of this angel in disguise, but I do know he did what he did as a volunteer, making his appearance three times a day. This was the very first time I had needed to be hospitalized in all the years I had lived in England. Like most people, I had a secret dread of ever having to go there.

On this occasion I was away from my present home in America; it was a little daunting for me to wake up in hospital on my first day in England. There was nothing to dread; I know the warmth which came from that dear senior citizen as he served "a cuppa tea, luv" went a great way towards my recovery.

# Chapter 15

## A Way of Life

I have to write that the presence of tea in England is all pervading. I can't imagine any home in England which does not own at least one teapot. It is quite possible to be anywhere almost and be able to enjoy a cup of tea. I have been considering various occasions and venues when tea is part, and sometimes a dominant part of the event.

We have the Duchess of Bedford to thank for the institution of "Afternoon Tea". It was customary for aristocrats to have their evening meal around 9.00 pm, the previous meal being at 12 noon. That was a long time in between, you must agree. The Duchess, tired of being tormented by hunger pains, decided to do something about it by instructing her servant to secretly prepare her tea and some dainties to eat along with the tea. This was so enjoyable that before she realized, it had become a habit. She could not contain her delight and began to share it by inviting her friends along to enjoy her new found freedom.

Soon this delightful experience became popular and became known as "Afternoon Tea". It is characterized by its elegance and grace. It could be said that Caesar Ritz drew his inspiration from this already established tradition. Certainly it has produced many happy and memorable occasions when ladies have loved the opportunity for either giving or being invited to an afternoon tea.

I have to concede that a genuine afternoon tea is less of an occasion in Britain nowadays, due to the changes in the structure of its social life. As a result, I think the genuine "Afternoon Tea" experience has a higher value and brings a great deal of pleasure. These days, I have found that people take tea more seriously than say, a few years ago, when it was an every day occurrence. By serious, I do not mean solemn but authentic. This means, of course, dressing up appropriately, even to wearing a hat and gloves.

The hostess would go to great lengths to ensure everything was just perfect, a pristine tablecloth, the finest of bone china and gleaming silver-ware. There would be the daintiest of sandwiches cut paper thin, delicious scones, possibly with strawberries and clotted cream, and a few exquisite tiny cakes decorated in a variety of ways.

You would not normally leave the table feeling ready to burst, as afternoon tea is supposed to be a repast until dinner. Do you know what I think? Sometimes rules are meant to be bent a little, and truth is, that usually when you have had afternoon tea, you do not even want dinner later on.

I would have to say that the tea-kettle is the most widely used utensil in an average English household. Tea is served for breakfast, midmorning, lunch, afternoon, teatime and suppertime. Days have long vanished when one had to wait quite a time for the cast-iron tea-kettle to boil on the coal fire. Most of the kettle's surface would be well blackened from being on the fire so much, but a portion around the top would be kept shiny by the use of black-lead. It was always a cheering sight to see the kettle on the fire sitting cozily on the burning coals and to await, in anticipation, the sound as it came to a rolling boil, emitting a generous stream of powerful white steam.

Nowadays, of course, most kitchens are equipped either with a kettle that sits on the stove or with one of the numerous models of electric kettle which has the advantage of being quick to the boil. In England it is a hallmark of hospitality to offer visitors a cup of tea. Usually the kettle would be put on before you were even asked if you would like tea. There have been times when it has been remarked that on entering a person's house, "they were not offered a cup of tea". This could indicate the visitor was not really welcome. I choose to believe this only happened on a very rare occasion.

# Chapter 16

## Other Customs and Practices

### Shouting out cake

In the North of England where I come from, there was a custom which was called the "shouting out cake". You may think what has that to do with tea?

Years before I was born in 1919 and even several years after my son was born in 1941, it was customary to have your baby born at home with the help of a midwife. All of this would need a lot of preparation in advance. One of the things to be prepared was a rich fruit cake. This was to ensure there would be something good to eat after the baby was born and the mother was made comfortable.

As soon as the baby arrived, word was spread quickly to waiting husband, mother and everyone else who had anything to do with the baby's birth. Hence the cake became known as the "shouting out cake", referring to everyone shouting out the news of the birth. By this time everyone concerned would be very tired and most of all glad, so it didn't take long to have the kettle boiling and a good strong cup of tea brewed to be enjoyed with the "shouting out cake".

### Tea on tap

I very much doubt this custom is carried out, except maybe in very rural areas. This custom continued into the early years of my married life, which began in 1940. I always thoroughly enjoyed participating in the custom I am going to describe.

This was the time before thermos flasks were used by people in general and before tea bags became popular. Barely a week would pass without either a gang of workmen or tradesmen and sometimes gypsies or tramps would knock on your door asking for boiling water to make their tea. You would be presented with a pint mug with a mashing of tea in the bottom. All they wanted was for you to fill up their mug with boiling water. This they would take and squat down somewhere against a wall, enjoying their sandwiches and a freshly brewed mug of tea. I think you will be getting the message that the English do like their tea made fresh and have never really taken kindly to thermos flasks.

I see here a beautiful faith lesson for us; there is just nothing to be compared to having a fresh daily time with our Heavenly Father. Sometimes, like the thermos flask, which is second best, circumstances prevent us from our treasured time with God. At least we know He is still with us.

# Chapter 17

## Tea on the beach

Yes, tea on the beach! It was quite a customary thing for us to pack up a picnic on those occasions when we would go to the beach. This would include packing our small stove, which had been bought at the Woolworth's store for sixpence, a tin kettle for quick boiling and a teapot.

It was always a good feeling to be squatted down on the beach, waiting with joyful anticipation for the split second when the water would arrive at the rolling boil. You know by now that a "rolling boil" is a phrase I dearly love. It conjures up the pure ecstasy which one receives from a cup of tea correctly made English fashion.

We never considered this procedure a chore, but rather one of delight bringing with it its own aura and sense of well being. We usually went this way when we took up our position on the beach in a secluded area, far away from any sign of commercialism.

In general, it is always possible to have tea available on the normal crowded areas of the beach. I know that nowadays, tea is served in Styrofoam cups, but it is still good tea for all that.

I have a very amusing story to tell you from bygone days when tea at the beach was served up in porcelain mugs. This happened approximately in the year 1950 on the small sandy beach in Folkestone, Kent. Here we had a very crowded beach, mainly because on that part of the coast the beaches were mostly pebbly. Above the beach was a promenade and under this were a series of arches. The children used the arches as a changing area before they went into the sea.

We were with friends and our respective sons on this particular day. As usual, the portion of beach was crowded as it was a very hot sunny day. My husband and our friends were fast asleep in their deck chairs whilst our sons were enjoying themselves in the sea. Suddenly I became aware of a man picking his way very gingerly through the mass of legs sticking out of deck chairs, carrying a tray with several mugs of steaming hot tea. That job alone took a lot of maneuvering and not everyone was in a hurry to volunteer for such a hazardous task of getting from tea kiosk to beach without a mishap.

My attention was briefly distracted from watching the struggling tea bearer by a strident voice calling out, "Here y'are, Johnnie, here's ya shoes." The voice came from immediately above where I was sitting. At the very same instant, there was our tea bearer, and wallop, Johnnie's shoes landed right on the tea bearer's tray. If only that moment could have been caught on camera. In one glance, to see the mugs of tea rise and fall spilling a considerable amount of tea, the total look of shock and embarrassment on the woman's face and to see little Johnnie emerge from his position under the arches where he had been changing and now not knowing what to do, was a scene I am never likely to forget.

But what of our tea bearer and how did he react to this incredible incident? Well, in the mildest manner, he looked up at the woman, and then very calmly continued his precarious passage towards his destination. I had my own reaction to this astonishing episode, that of uncontrollable laughter. It did not help me as I viewed my sleeping companions, who had missed witnessing what surely must be considered a once in a life time happening.

*Dolly's husband George making tea on the beach*

*Dolly's husband George and brother-in-law
enjoy tea on the beach*

# Chapter 18

## Before the tea bag

As a child I have vivid recollections of friends and relatives of my parents visiting us. Often these visits would be just casual, so of course, there had been no elaborate preparations. This was never a problem to my mother who, "quick as greased lightning" would have afternoon tea laid out. This could be anything from a biscuit or cake, or if nothing else, out would come the bread and jam.

It was quite a common practice to tell fortunes from the tea leaves left at the bottom of the cup. We know the correct thing would have been to strain the tea as it was poured from the pot. That would automatically eliminate the fun that could be derived from the tea leaves left in the cup.

When friends had finished drinking their tea, sometimes they would say, "Let's tell our fortunes." To do this the dregs at the bottom of the cup would be sharply swirled around and then with dexterous movement, quickly upturned onto the saucer. The cup would be turned right side up and everyone would be peering into the cup with bated breath to see what pattern had emerged. Each pattern had a significant meaning, some of which are as follows:

- Leaves near the handle indicate the present time.
- Leaves near the rim indicate an event in the immediate future.
- Leaves near the bottom indicate an event in the future.
- Leaves in a straight line indicate a journey.

- Leaves in the shape of a star indicate the fulfilling of one's greatest hope.
- Leaves in the shape of trees and flowers indicate good luck.
- Leaves in the shape of clouds and serpents are bad omens.
- Leaves in the shape of a heart near the rim indicate love and happiness.

I very much doubt if anyone does this any more because people mostly use tea bags. It was really only a bit of harmless fun and I'm sure no one ever took it seriously. I have never done it myself and have no intentions of ever doing it, but I do wish to record everything I know about tea.

I know that several songs have been written which have Tea in their title. To quote but a few: "I like a nice cup of tea in the morning", "Tea for Two" and "Tea in Chicago". I know of at least one movie with tea in its title, "Tea with Mussolini". I recall going to this movie.

# Everything Stops for the Tea

Every nation in creation has its favourite drink
France is famous for its wine, it's beer in Germany
Turkey has its coffee and they serve it blacker than ink
Russians go for vodka and England loves its tea

Oh, the factories may be roaring
With a boom-a-lacka, zoom-a-lacka, wee
But there isn't any roar when the clock strikes four
Everything stops for tea

Oh, a lawyer in the courtroom
In the middle of an alimony plea
Has to stop and help 'em pour when the clock strikes four
Everything stops for tea

It's a very good English custom
Though the weather be cold or hot
When you need a little pick-up, you'll find a little tea cup
Will always hit the spot

You remember Cleopatra
Had a date to meet Mark Anthony at three
When he came an hour late she said "You'll have to wait"
For everything stops for tea

Oh, they may be playing football
And the crowd is yelling "Kill the referee!"
But no matter what the score, when the clock strikes four
Everything stops for tea

Oh, the golfer may be golfing
And is just about to make a hole-in-three
But it always gets them sore when the clock yells "four!"
Everything stops for tea

It's a very good English custom
And a stimulant for the brain
When you feel a little weary, a cup'll make you cheery
And it's cheaper than champagne

*Before the tea bag*

Now I know just why Franz Schubert
Didn't finish his unfinished symphony
He might have written more but the clock struck four
And everything stops for tea


Featured in Buchanan's 1935 comedy film,
"Come Out Of The Pantry"
(Goodhart / Hoffman / Sigler)
Jack Buchanan

# Chapter 19

## Everyday Tea Time

This is how you could be expected to take afternoon tea in a middle class household.

It is presented in an elegant way, bone china, pristine lace or embroidered table cloth and tiny serviettes. The basic food is wafer thin sliced brown and white bread and butter. In addition, there would be a selection of homemade jams and lemon curd served in special dishes. Maybe there would be cake or scones. This is the usual fare, even on Sundays and special days.

In the very first weeks of our marriage my husband and I were invited to tea on a holiday Sunday to the home of a wealthy middle-class family. As we were both from working class families we had no idea what to expect. I was feeling quite nervous at the prospect, even though I knew the people to be very gracious. At holiday time it was my family's custom to depart from the usual tea time fare and have a very grand spread. Naturally I was conjuring up in my mind just how grand an affair awaited us on our visit.

I was certainly in for a big surprise, not at the lavishness of the meal but at its simplicity. There we had it, brown bread and butter with home-made jam followed by Madeira cake. There was the silver tea service and the bone china, all very relaxing and elegant. There was no sense of embarrassment at all, serving this simple fare.

On the occasions we invited people to tea on special days we always made a "big spread". We would have been embarrassed not to have done. Incidentally, we always made a "big spread" on special days whether we had visitors or not.

I have written this to illustrate the variety of ways tea can be served, but as I often repeat, the defining factor is always the presence of authentic tea. This leads me to think of our Heavenly Father who is never tied down to places or circumstances but has His own way of invading our lives, regardless of the strata of society to which we belong.

# Chapter 20

# Tea Time Specials

## High Tea

There is a diversity of opinion as to the meaning of "High Tea". The opposite of anything high is obviously low, so let's start there. The "low" would not mean low tea; in fact I wouldn't even know anything about low tea, so I can't explain it. I believe it refers to the kind of table on which tea can be served. We have all seen a low table which usually occupies a place in the center of the sitting room. It is mostly referred to as a coffee table.

From earliest times when it became customary to serve tea early in the afternoon, it was usually set out on a low coffee table. This way the guests would sit around on comfortable chairs and sofas, helping themselves or being helped by the hostess to tea and dainties. Sometimes an array of dainty sandwiches would also be available.

There could be times when for the sake of convenience the repast would be laid out on a dining table, thus the expression was birthed, "High Tea". This expression simply referred to the height of the table, not its contents. "High Tea" has a totally new meaning now. I do not know just when "High Tea" became other than a table higher than a low table, but I do know that "High Tea" has been in existence all through my life time, which is considerably long.

Should you be invited to High Tea whilst in England, you would know that you would be receiving a very substantial meal. Normally, afternoon tea is served between 3 and 4 o'clock and is a very light meal. Everything is presented in a delicate dainty fashion.

The high tea, as we know it in Britain, is a very substantial meal. Usually it would be laid out on a brightly colored checked table-cloth. The tea would be brewed in a large brown teapot. Regular cups and saucers or even mugs would be used. Depending on the time of year, the main fare could be hot or cold. During the colder days anything from fish and chips or mixed grill could be served. On warmer days, ham or salmon salads could be served.

There would be an array of scones, tea-cakes and possibly fruit cake. One could also expect apple pie or some other fruit pie served with custard. It can best be described as a hearty meal and it served very well to satisfy the hunger of the working man. Sometimes this would be called a tea-dinner; tea would be served throughout the entire meal. It is quite opposite to afternoon tea, but each serves its own special function.

## Garden Parties

The English have always enjoyed taking tea outside. One of the events in rural English life which still endures is the vicarage garden party. In years gone by vicarages used to be very large with correspondingly spacious grounds, making them ideal places for summer garden parties.

These would take weeks of forward planning to ensure smooth running on the day. The majority of bread, cakes, jams, pastries and scones would be made by hand. Tables would be set out as elegantly as if tea was being served indoors. Guests would arrive duly attired in decorative hats and floral dresses. Often there would be stalls where you could purchase home-made jams, cakes etc.

## Strawberry Teas

Strawberry teas are very popular in England during the strawberry season. There can be nothing tasting better than freshly picked English strawberries. Strawberry teas usually comprise nothing else but strawberries served with clotted Devonshire or Cornish cream on top of scones, alongside a generous pot of freshly brewed tea.

Strawberry teas can occur anywhere, sometimes in the privacy of your own back garden with family or friends. Garden parties are a popular venue when the public is invited. A charge is usually made to cover costs, but often times these are fund raising functions so people are encouraged to be generous. Tea is available throughout the event, thus making everyone feel contented.

The most famous strawberry cream teas, of course, are the Cornish Cream Teas and the Devonshire Cream Teas. The special clotted cream they use on the strawberries is the reason for their popularity. It has to be fresh for maximum enjoyment and so the only way to achieve this is to take a trip to Devon or Cornwall. It is possible to purchase this cream from the stores, but because it is treated to keep for a certain number of days it loses its distinctive taste.

## Winter Teas

Winter teas are so cozy. Certainly they are a rarity these days, if not totally extinct. The prime necessity is a huge roaring fire. An open hearth, the day is short, the curtains drawn, the large black kettle humming a cheerful song as it comes to the boil, table and chairs pulled up close, what could be better? Now the fun part starts. Maybe two people at once with muffins impaled on their toasting forks begin toasting these till they turn a nut-brown color. Straight away they butter the muffins lavishly and maybe spread with a generous portion of jam. Then a strong cup of tea is poured to complete this fine fare.

One doesn't have to have muffins to enjoy this repast; thick slices of home-made bread would be good. To have a winter tea in this way can be so relaxing that it can take away any inclination to get down to homework or anything else that needs to be done, and before you know, it has you fast asleep. Such is the power of winter tea time.

## The Nursery Tea

It seems that even very small children were introduced to the art and pleasure of taking tea. In very high society young children were trained mostly by nannies and governesses. This meant that most of their time was spent in the nursery. This of course, did not apply to ordinary children, who were allowed to mingle freely with the rest of the family.

One thing they did have in common was their early introduction to the beverage, tea. This tea became known as Calico Tea. This was because it was made up of a small amount of tea and lots of milk, thus taking on the color of calico. Also children would be served with dainty finger-like sandwiches, the fillings being of a simpler type than those served to adults. Even so, at a very early age children acquired both the art and love of taking tea.

Here is a simple faith lesson; no one is ever too young to be introduced to the love and knowledge of God. He can be understood and a love for Him can grow as the years move on.

# Chapter 21

## Tea in times of need and celebration

Tea always shows up in times of celebration and times of disaster. It was a well known scene during the frequent air-raids which occurred in England during World War II. Booths already pouring out steaming hot cups of sweet tea seemed to appear from nowhere, as if by magic. They were manned by the Salvation Army, the Red Cross and others. Their very presence just seemed to bring an aura of stability, which was greatly needed at such times.

The same thing would occur whenever there was a pit disaster or any similar calamity. Somehow, there just seems to be something therapeutic about the very sight of a cup of tea. It seems to produce a feeling of solidarity and comfort, breaking down social barriers to produce a sense of unity and camaraderie.

As a child I have witnessed scenes of distress at the coal mine head on receiving the calamitous news that there had been an underground explosion. One can feel the anguish in the air as loved ones kept their vigil for any reassuring news that their loved one may be safe. At such times the inevitable tea canteens would be in full swing. Groups would be gathered together holding on to mugs of tea, each held tightly with two hands as if clutching hold of any hope there may be of a loved one's survival. An arm would be extended around a stooped shoulder to convey a little strength, hope and care. The vigil could be long and the atmosphere somber, but always at hand was the comforting cup of tea.

In complete contrast, people of England just love an occasion for a communal celebration. These celebrations are usually in the form of a communal tea party. Disasters always come without warning, but celebrations are very different because a date is decided on, well ahead of time.

The usual reasons for these communal celebrations are the end of a war, a reigning monarch's coronation or jubilee. These are national celebrations, but at any time a town or village could have a communal tea party for a variety of reasons. This kind of celebration would take much time and forward planning and everyone would hope for favorable weather.

Communal celebrations were held outdoors, tables being set out all the way down the street. Families would all bring their contributions of sandwiches, cakes and scones. Of course, the one and only beverage served was tea. They were joyous occasions, certainly not elaborate, but most definitely creating an atmosphere of congeniality.

## Tea in times of need and celebration

THIS ENGLAND, *Autumn, 2008*

▷ *An extremely rare colour picture of a WRVS tea car serving ARP workers in a bombed out town. The YMCA Women's Auxiliary and other comparable groups wore similar uniforms but with a distinctive arm band. However, because of black and white photography, confusion still reigns so if anyone is aware of any other colour images of wartime women's uniforms then please let us know.*

*Courtesy of "This England Magazine"*
*Volunteers serving tea in a bombed out town in*
*Britain during WWII*

# Chapter 22

## Top to Bottom

It's funny, but there are times when we associate food and drink with certain events which happen to us in our life. I well remember having the best cup of coffee in my life in Kennedy Airport. Why would it taste so good? For the simple reason, we were on our way home to England after having visited our son and his family in U.S.A. and after experiencing all the joy of being with them, I now felt really sad inside at having to part. I particularly recall enjoying a cup of coffee like I have never enjoyed one before or since.

I cannot recall any one occasion when having a cup of tea stands out more than any other. Many times I have been proverbially "dying for a cup of tea". Surely there is one place to have a cup of tea that would stay fixed in my memory and that place would be Buckingham Palace. There is no likelihood that opportunity would ever come my way. I would like to write about it, but I cannot write from experience because I have not been invited. However, I know personally a gentleman who has been there; in fact he was dubbed Sir John.

Tea with the Queen at Buckingham Palace takes place during the summer and is held outdoors in the gardens. It is, of course, by invitation only. The guests come from all walks of life and are carefully chosen for some outstanding achievement or some good work they have done within the community. Attendees are well briefed ahead of time on the correct attire and how to respond to Her Majesty when being presented. It is a standing up occasion and can be very long. Usually a glimpse of the Queen is brief, but brief it may be, the memory of it will remain forever.

I understand the tea itself is very simple and traditional, comprising cucumber sandwiches cut paper thin, followed by scones, strawberries and cream. There could be cakes, I don't know, but I do know there was plenty of tea and this was a tea the guests would never ever forget.

Obviously the whole event for the guest will have taken hours of preparation, making sure they wore suitable attire. The long journey to Buckingham Palace, standing in line, as part of a large crowd waiting to be personally greeted by Her Majesty, tasting the food and drinking her tea, all part of an event which would be retold to family and friends for a very long time. Who can blame them? Surely they had a cup of tea to remember.

Now we will take a dive to the low point. It is the place where tea is the vital element for the occasion. I have in my mind an indelible picture of a miner walking down the street on his way to begin his shift down the coal mine. This was in the days before pits were equipped with showers, so miners went to work in the clothes they would wear underground. Around his waist was a belt. Strung on the belt were his snap tin and his "dudley". The snap tin was so shaped that it would be impossible for a rat to prize it open and consume the miner's lunch of the traditional jam and bread. The "dudley", or you may be more familiar with the word "canteen", was filled with, yes, you have already guessed, cold tea. This very simple and basic fare of tea and bread and jam was proved to be most practical and suitable in such working conditions.

So we see our miner with canteen and snap tin flapping from his belt, getting closer to the pit head. I wonder what his thoughts are as he leaves the sunlight to be lowered deep into the mine and crawls on hands and knees to his place of toil. Let's try to take a glimpse of our miner in our mind's eye, as he takes time out for his "snap". Often times he would be quite alone, his only light being that of his carbon lamp, which would be strapped around his forehead. By now he will have discarded all his clothes apart from his pit "hockers", in other words, baggy shorts.

Hopefully he will be able to locate the spot where he deposited his lunch, knowing that it was impossible for rats to break into his snap tin. Probably he would reach for his "dudley" first and take a really long drink. Oh, what rapture! No place to wash hands or take a walk, just crouched there in the darkness with only the flickering light from his helmet, which on occasion would reveal the eyes of a waiting rat, hoping to snatch the smallest crumb which could fall.

After the bread and jam our miner would once again reach for his canteen of tea. It was so cold, maybe have some sugar in it, but oh, how refreshing. Over time there must have been gallons of tea drunk down the mines and every drink a drink to be remembered. I'm sure if our miner had the choice of taking tea down the mine or taking tea at Buckingham Palace he would choose the latter. On the other hand, if you asked him which he needed most, obviously his answer would be when he was deep in the bowels of the earth.

From these two life pictures I see a great life lesson. In both instances tea is the most important element and we need to recognize who or what is most important to us. We all have our high points and we all have our low points. There is Someone who is reaching out to us with the promise that He will never leave us or forsake us. In our high times we tend to forget that He is still the one who is there, but in the low times we are brought to realize just how much we need that Someone, who promised never to leave us nor forsake us.

Tea has been around for a long time and we could say it is here to stay. Similarly God is eternal, without beginning and without end. This same eternal God extends His love to us all through His only begotten Son, Jesus Christ and tells us He loves us with an everlasting love and says to us, "Lo, I am with you always, even to the end of the world."

I do not remember my very first cup of tea. But one thing I do know is that I have been drinking tea as far back as my memory takes me. I expect I will go on enjoying drinking tea to the end of my days, except if I am unable to procure tea any more, but I hope this is highly unlikely.

I am now at the end of my meanderings on the subject of tea, but that does not in any way imply that I have written all that can be written about this subject. I am sure there must be reams more to discover. This leads me into my last faith lesson. Who is there who can't recall the scripture which says about Solomon, "the half has never been told"? I remember vividly when I first came to know my Creator as revealed through His Son, Jesus Christ. My heart was filled with awe and wonder, and even this present day, some 74 years later, my heart and mind are still amazed at the awesomeness of my Great God and Savior.

Throughout the years my taste for authentic tea has never diminished; in an even greater way my thirst and passion for the living God has never diminished, but rather increases with each passing year.

Let me conclude with some words from Psalm 34 and verse 8. "O taste and see that the Lord is good." Here are some words from the lips of Jesus, "If anyone is thirsty, let him come to me and drink. Whoever believes in me, as the scripture has said, streams of living water will flow out of him." (John 7 v 37 – 38) There is no way this living water will ever, ever run dry.

*Illustrated by Cliff Baxendale*
*A welcome repast for the miner*

# Post Script

## Your Tea Party Formula

If you have never yet embarked on the adventure of presenting a tea party yourself, I'm sure that after reading this book, a desire will have been kindled within you to step into the untried. I can assure you that if you follow the formula I have laid out you will not find it daunting at all. It will be a challenge for you as you move into uncharted territory. Your sense of achievement, satisfaction and joy will be more than reward for your bravery.

I have divided the formula into 3 parts: 1) Planning 2) Preparation 3) Pleasurable Participation

### 1) Planning

Decide on the time, date and venue.

Consider whom you would invite; a party of eight works well.

Determine which kind of table linen you will use and the type of flowers.

Think about the variety of sandwiches, cakes and scones you will serve.

### 2) Preparation

Send out invitations in reasonable time.

Check out the table linen, china ware etc.

Make sure everything is clean and the silver is polished.

Bake ahead of time those pastries and cakes which can be frozen.

The day before, clean the house, set out your table.

Make sure you have supplies of tea, sugar and milk to hand.

The night before, prepare the fillings for the sandwiches.
The morning of the tea party, arrange fresh flowers.
Make the sandwiches and cover with a damp cloth and refrigerate.
Bake the fresh scones.
After lunch set everything out, shower and glamorize yourself.

## 3) Pleasurable Participation

As you await the arrival of your guests, already your home will have an air of peace as you sit gracefully in an armchair, looking as if you have never had any hustle or bustle in presenting this beautiful tea. If you follow my formula you will be spared all the hassle which could result from not planning and being prepared ahead of time.

As your guests arrive they should be captivated by the sheer charm, elegance and tranquility of the occasion. They will want to know the secret of your success. You have the formula: plan, prepare and pleasurable participation.

We all need times set apart to be still and calm so that our inner self may be renewed by our Creator. He has much to say to us if only we would choose to lay aside time to listen for His voice. Truly He holds the key to enduring peace.

*Dolly's granddaughter Miriam is ready to receive her guests*

# Endnotes

The source of my "fair use" information in chapter 5 came from the London Ritz Book of Afternoon Tea By, Helen Simpson, publisher Arbor House, New York 1986

Camellia Sinensis information, chapter 2 came from James A Duke, Handbook of Energy Crops 1983 unpublished

Health Benefits, Source Health Benefits, US News and World Report, Feb 7, 2000 chapter 2

Ritz Tea, Chapter 13, some of this information came from Wikipedia Free Encyclopedia Article ID # 1506442 "Hotel Ritz Paris

Opium Wars Chapter 7. Source The Opium Wars by Edgar Hole, Pulman 1964, Wikipedia Free Encyclopedia

*Photo of Author*

# About the Author

Dolly Yates was born Dorothy Mary Robson the third daughter to Tot & Ina Robson on August 30, 1919 in Durham County, England. She grew up in a working class family and loved going to school.

The age of 14 was a turning point for Dolly when she responded to the claim of Christ on her life. From a young teenager she began speaking in public about her faith and continues to this day. She married her only sweetheart George in 1940, and a son was born in 1941. When her son Paul grew he married and shortly after came to live with his wife in the U.S.A.

In her thirties she learned to play the piano. In her forties she took up swimming. In her fifties she began painting and horseback riding. She became a widow in her sixties, during which time she adjusted and came to live with son Paul and his wife in America (where she later became an official US citizen in 2005). Her seventies found her taking a missions trip to the Philippines and in her eighties we find her learning to use the computer and writing this, her first book.

She is the beloved mother of one son, three granddaughters, and 11 great grandchildren. She is affectionately known as "Granma Dolly" by all who have the joy of knowing her. She still keeps very active in many areas, and we all look forward to see what she decided to take on in her nineties!

# Index